# Symphonies

*The third poetic collection*

*by*

*Esperanza Habla*

© 2017 La Luna Press

ISBN: 978-0-9915104-7-4

Library of Congress Control Number: 2017935521

Cover design and all photographs by Esperanza Habla
Author portrait courtesy of Kristen Pugh Photography
Logo for La Luna Press by Adam Whitaker

All rights reserved. No part of this publication may be reproduced, distributed, or transmitted in any form or by any means, including photocopying, recording, or other electronic or mechanical methods, without the prior written permission of the publisher, except in the case of brief quotations embodied in critical reviews and certain other noncommercial uses permitted by copyright law.

For permission requests, write to the publisher, at the address below.

La Luna Press, L.L.C.
P.O. Box 533284
Indianapolis, IN
46253
USA

Thank you for purchasing this book.

For more information, please visit us at:

www.lalunapress.com

Thank you to my dear family for their love and support:

Amy, David, Debbie, Diane, Hope, John, Johnny, Kristi, Marjorie, Megan, Wayne

I would like take a moment to personally
thank the music professors, vocal coaches,
teachers and choir directors I trained with
as a singer, performer and an artist:

Keys, Hannah, Carey, Lineback, Rice,
Wagner, Miller, Tucker, Reid,
Larner, Gallagher, Fox, Leffler,
Kern, and Largent

You taught me to see the beauty in music,
in performing, in art, in life,
and most of all,
in myself.

Thank you.

## Table of Contents:

| | |
|---|---|
| My Day.................................. | 1 |
| Adorable Sight....................... | 2 |
| The Name of the Game.................... | 4 |
| Symphonies......................... | 6 |
| Life Altering Changes....................... | 7 |
| A Letter to the Little Prince............. | 8 |
| Nighttime Cacophony....................... | 11 |
| Indulgent............................ | 12 |
| Lunar Goddess.............................. | 13 |
| Peace..................................... | 15 |
| Equality................................. | 17 |
| Pursuit of Beauty............................ | 20 |
| Misconceptions......................... | 22 |
| Glorious Sky........................... | 26 |
| Mask of the Moon........................... | 27 |
| It Was Fifty Years Ago Today............ | 29 |
| A Grateful Heart............................ | 31 |
| The Meaning of Life........................ | 34 |
| The Act of Comparison..................... | 37 |
| It Was Not My Time......................... | 40 |
| Visible........................ | 45 |
| Friendship, Love, Sex, Truth, Lies, Hope, Hate and the Internet.... | 48 |
| I Know................................... | 52 |
| Another Day is Done......................... | 53 |
| Alike..................................... | 55 |
| Lonely Fedora................................ | 59 |
| The Birth of a Book........................ | 60 |
| The Heart.............................. | 62 |
| Scars and Storms............................ | 63 |
| Tolerance................................. | 65 |

*Symphonies*

# My Day                                  May 15, 2013

*An internal monologue

(Yawn)

Oh, I am exhausted. I barely got any sleep. Stupid kittens.

No, I should not say that. I love the kittens. I just do not love the hours they keep. Let me go feed them.....

I am so tired. Well, I should get ready for work. Let me get my bath water started.....

Oooh, this hot water feels so good. It is so restorative.
I could stay in here all day.

Darn it, I was going to wash my hair. Maybe I still can, if I lean back in the water.....

Ohhhhhh, this feels so good. It feels good to float in the water. I could stay here all day.

I hear my heartbeat in my ears; it reverberates through the water.

This is beyond luxurious. I could stay here all day.
(yawn)

But I can't. There are things I need to do.
(yawn)

I'd better get ready for my day.

## Adorable Sight  May 16, 2013

This morning, while running an errand, I saw two Canada geese walking across the road. A line of cars quickly formed behind the geese, who were dawdling on their way. They were not in any hurry to cross that road.

It was amusing to see all of the cars lined up, stopped in the road, for two Canada geese. While watching the geese cross, and the growing line of cars, I thought to myself, "Why would geese be here? There's no water nearby. Why would the geese be here?" In a moment I would have my answer.

I arrived at my destination and found myself looking at a truly adorable sight. Just ahead, behind a gas station, in a patch of grass, I saw two adult Canada geese and about 12 goslings. The goslings were adorable. They were very little, with fluffy grey feathers. They were almost little fluff balls with beaks sticking out.

Now I knew why the Canada geese had been crossing the road; they were en route to their babies, who were close by, being watched by friends or relatives.

Looking at the gaggle of geese, it looked like a geese play date. One adult goose watched over six or so of the goslings as they grazed in the grass. Another adult goose was under a small tree, in the shade, sitting under a tree, watching the rest of the goslings, which were resting peacefully.

Suddenly, a gust of wind came out of nowhere; the goslings' new feathers danced in the breeze. The babies shuddered in the sudden cold. It was beyond cute.

*Symphonies*

Here, in the middle of the city, I found two families of Canada geese, making themselves home on a bit of grass behind a gas station. I found it odd to find such a sight in an urban landscape.

It made nervous to see them in such an area, surrounded by busy roads full of cars and trucks. It also made me hopeful that the geese could find the green space down the road, with a mini pond attached, where they would be out of harm's way. It made me think of that quote from that famous dinosaur movie: "Nature finds the way."

I took a picture of the family of geese before I left; you will find the two adult Canada geese and a few of the goslings in the photo below. There's not much else to say about encountering this gaggle of geese. It was truly an adorable sight.

*"Canada Goose Family" by Esperanza Habla*

*Symphonies*

## The Name of the Game          May 19, 2013

Being a poet has been a very eye opening experience for me. I have met many fellow artists in my writing career, from a myriad of art forms. I recently had a conversation with a friend of mine, a photographer, who has pages for her photography business in various social media outlets.

We spoke about art and promoting oneself as an artist. She made the point that she occasionally feels that, posting her latest work on her photography page, makes her feel that others will view her as being self-involved or self-obsessed; in reality, nothing could be further from the truth.

Listening to her voice these concerns made complete sense to me. I have felt this way upon occasion. It is a delicate balance, to let people know about your art, your latest pieces, what you're currently working on, and what projects you will launch in the future, and to not be thought of as being self-involved.

Too often, responses from posts can act as a form of validation. It's almost like the artist is jumping up and down, furiously waving their arms, screaming:

> *"Look over here! Look at me! I just did something awesome! I just put out a book! I just put out an album! I have a new movie coming out! I have a gallery opening this weekend! Please come find me! Click 'like'! Share through every social media platform there is!"*

In these days of constant feed from social media, self-promotion is the name of the game. Anyone doing business must utilize this tool: artists, doctors, lawyers, small business owners, entrepreneurs.

Self-promotion is important to help the artist connect to their audience, the small business owner to their clients and customers.

As artists, we need to learn to utilize this tool.

Sharing your art, posting a recent project, sharing an upcoming event, should never be seen as being self-involved or self-obsessed.

It is simply self-promotion.

# Symphonies                                    May 21, 2013

Once you meet a true writer, you know. You can tell by the way they speak. They speak in poetry. Sonorous words drip from their tongues like succulent honey. Their words are notes in a glorious symphony. Some poets and authors write to express themselves. Other authors write for their readers. Others write because they have to. That's what we do. Writers write.
For me, when I write poetry, it is to express myself, to talk about things that are important to me, or to discuss an issue I'm passionate about. I am also writing my first novel: "Samantha." When I write in the book, it is different. I am writing it because I have a story to tell. I have more stories in my head right now. I hope to tell all of my stories. I hope to thus, one day, be a professional storyteller. I do not write melodies or speak in poetry. One could argue therefore that I am not a true writer. I challenge that thought. I was born with this gift, and only discovered it three years ago. I am an apprentice, still learning my craft. I have time to learn. I have time to ply my craft, to tell my stories, to write my melodies, compose my symphonies.

*"Symphonies" by Esperanza Habla*

# Life Altering Changes          May 26, 2013

Many things have changed in the last week, in the lives of many of my friends. Some of the changes were joyous and exciting, some terrifying and sorrowful. All were life altering.

I do not like negative changes. Many of us feel that way. Often we do not like change because we are challenged by it. It takes us out of our comfort zones; it shows our lack of control. It is an uncomfortable realization.

All of the changes in the lives of my friends, be they joyful or sorrowful, were equal in their intensities. Hearing all of these life altering changes proved to be too much for me.
I found that I had to disconnect from the world for an hour or two, and recharge my personal energies.

At first, I felt overwhelmed, hearing about the sorrowful, terrifying changes my friends had experienced. I felt powerless to help them in their time of need. But I was not powerless at all. I did the only thing I could do for my friends-I listened and I prayed.

Things will happen to us in our lives, both joyous and terrifying. Sometimes these changes will alter our lives. In the face of such changes, we must remember that we have a choice in how we react to them. We can embrace the joyous changes, pray about the sorrowful, and be there for one another when these life altering changes occur.

*Symphonies*

## A Letter to the Little Prince          June 3, 2013

*\*A few years ago, I met a Little Prince. Not that Little Prince- a Little Clown Prince. This letter is to him.*

Hello little prince, my mime friend. We have not talked in quite a while. I trust you are well. How are you enjoying life in the United States? One of your friends informed me that you are living here now. I hope you are having a smooth transition. I had the chance to see the movie you were in-about the woman who fishes. I will soon be receiving the DVD. It is truly a beautiful film, both visually and in its message. I am proud to have been the first financial backer for the movie. I wish it continued success. I recently received a message from your friend V. She showed me your latest movie trailer, for the movie you made with her. I remember when you let me read the script, to get my input on the project. I wish you a successful premiere.

A few months ago, a friend of yours brought one of your films to my attention. You will know which film it is-the title is my name. I later spoke to Papa C about it. He was so excited about the project; he thought it was a collaborative project between you and I. I informed him that that was not the case. I watched the trailer you sent me, for your book. I was impressed. It is different from the original storyboard video you sent me. I was surprised to see my words in the trailer. I was surprised to see the words of Mr. C. as well. I hope sales are going well. I hope the world loves it as I do.

I remember reading the book, thinking that the book was a love letter to our friendship. I still feel the same way. Our friendship will live forever in this book. I am so proud that I inspired you to write the book. I am proud that I am in the book. It is the best birthday present I have ever received.

*Symphonies*

Like you once told me, without me, the book would not exist. I am proud that I was such a source of inspiration for you.

I have been writing as well. My poetry career has continued to grow. In fact, it has been so successful, I created my own website. In December of 2012 I created this new blog.
I decided to change blogs because the new blog formats offered a translation feature. Readers can pick a language from a list over 60 languages, and have my words translated into their language. There are no language barriers. Since the launch of the blog, my writings have become quite popular.
To date I have had over 7,600 visits to the site-which is about as many visitors as my first blog had in three years' time.
I average about 1,400 visits to the blog monthly. I have readers in over 30 countries. I have such a following now, I created a page in Facebook to share my poetry. I'm even on Twitter and LinkedIn now!

A few months ago I began to research how to publish my poetry. I decided that the best way to publish my poetry is to do it myself. I have created my own publishing company to publish my poems, and my novel. My company is called "La Luna Press." The books will literally be from the moon.
I created a website as well as a page in Facebook for La Luna Press. You should check it out. It must be such a sense of accomplishment, to finally have your book published. I will soon know that joy. My books of poetry are in the editing stages now. I will have 4 books available for purchase in print (two in Spanish, two in English), and will have the same 4 books available in an electronic book format. I will release 8 books my first year as a publisher! As I look to the future, I hope to publish the written works of other writers as well. There are many stories yet to be told. It is such an exciting time for me! I have a long list of labels-Esperanza Habla: Poet, Writer, Author, Translator, Small Business Owner, Publisher.

*Symphonies*

I heard a phrase the other day, a phrase which brought you to mind. It said:

> *"The deeper we fall in love,*
> *the more unlovable we behave."*

That phrase made me think of the end of our friendship. We would not have reacted the way we did if we were not dear friends, if we did not truly care about one another, and about one another's opinions. I regret the way things ended between us. However, I know it was for the best.

I do not know if you will remember, but we had many conversations throughout our friendship about promises. I still do not like promises. However, you kept a promise to me. I will now keep my promise to you.

My last promise.

Take care little prince, my mime friend. Take care and be well.

> *"He loved you enough to come in to your life*
> *so that you would learn what you needed to learn.*
> *Regardless of how he did it."*
> *-Iyanla Vanzant*

*Symphonies*

# Nighttime Cacophony  June 6, 2013

I have just gone to bed.

I have said my prayers.

I am ready to sleep.

I lay in bed, trying to quiet my brain.

At last, stillness comes. Serenity reigns.

Yet it is short-lived.

My ears hear and my brain registers the myriad of noises in the night....

Geese honking
frogs croaking
crickets chirping
water flowing in fountain in the duck pond
a car driving down my street
traffic from the nearby highway
a bird calling in the night
car horn blaring
water rushing through the pipes
kittens running like thundering stallions
car door slamming
people shouting
dogs barking
front door slamming
airplanes taking off

No wonder I can't sleep, with such cacophony.

## Indulgent

June 12, 2013

How indulgent reading is. The reader can open a book, an electronic book or magazine, a news report or blog, anywhere they want: in their living room, traveling by bus, relaxing on a mountaintop, in the bathtub. We the reader can read the encapsulated words at our leisure, any time, day or night. We can escape from our worlds and realities, lives and responsibilities, in the covers of a book.

The art of writing is also indulgent. Unlike other artists, the writer does not have to get an agent, get an audience, fill a theater, balance the sound and acoustics, perfect the lighting, have a photo shoot.

All a writer needs to create their art in the moment of creation is a visit from the muse known as inspiration, time alone with a pen and paper, or a computer and keyboard, a quiet place to think, or a room filled with music, the thoughts in their head and the courage to write.

Writing can also be self-indulgent; after a piece is written, the writer can then read the art they have just created. The writer becomes the reader, their own audience. Whether it is shared with the world or not, the art must be pleasing to only their eye.

I love sitting at a computer, alone with my thoughts, tapping into the creative force that runs through me. I can only create art at its highest level through my writing. I am grateful for the gift I have been given. It is my greatest indulgence.

# Lunar Goddess                       June 19, 2013

Yesterday, an online friend and fellow poet of the moon reached out to me. He mentioned that I am just like the Goddess Ixchel. I was glad for the compliment; however, I had no idea what he was talking about. He then sent me a link to a website that explained what he meant.

I clicked the link, and read the story of the Goddess Ixchel, the Goddess of the Moon, from Mexican mythology.
I thanked him for the immense compliment. After all, it is not every day that I am compared to a goddess.

I then began to research the legend and folklore of the goddess of the moon. I found some names I had heard of, many I had not, including Phoebe, Artemis, Menily, Hecate, Chia, Diana, Mano, to name a few. The Greek goddess of the moon is Selene; she is said to be the Greek personification of the moon.

The name I am familiar with is Luna, the Roman goddess of the moon. She is said to be the divine embodiment of the moon.

In researching goddesses of the moon, I learned that the moon is most often personified as a female deity, linking the phases of the moon to a woman's menstrual cycle.

Knowing that information, I was surprised to learn that there are gods of the moon, male deities to personify the moon, in some mythologies as well. Quite often, the sun is depicted as one sex, the moon as the opposite sex.

Sometimes they are depicted as mortal enemies, brother and sister, and even lovers.

## *Symphonies*

In reading about the lunar deities I was fascinated to learn that there is a system of gods and goddesses, from peoples and countries and cultures around the world, all of which are amazingly similar.

It probably dates back to the time of Pangaea, when the entire world had only one continent. How else could people in different places create similar folklores and mythologies?

Whatever the mythology, the story of the goddess, the origin of the myth, for me, the spirit of the moon is female. I think of the moon as Luna, the Roman name, the Spanish word.

I believe she is the one that comes to me, in a multitude of forms, a butterfly, a beam of moonlight, and gives me inspiration to write.

Do I believe I compare in any way to a goddess? No.

Do I know why my friend compared me to a lunar goddess? No.

I call myself "the poet of the moon."

Being a humble poet is hardly comparative to a goddess.

That being said, it is truly an honor to be compared to a goddess of any type.

Especially a lunar goddess.

# Peace  June 21, 2013

There is a concept I have been thinking about a lot lately-the concept of peace. Anyone that knows me can tell you that I have always identified with the "hippie movement", the culture and social change in America in the 1960s and 1970s, the music of that period, tie-dye, peace symbols, concepts of peace and love, psychedelic designs, bohemian colors.

In high school and college, I was often found wearing a tie-dye shirt or wearing a peace symbol medallion. For years I have drawn a peace symbol in my written correspondence, just after my name. It has become a signature. A co-worker joked with me once,
**"If I see a note with your name, and there is no peace symbol drawn on it, I know it is a forgery."**

Recently, I wore a scarf with peace symbols on it to a work function. A co-worker noticed the scarf and said,
**"Oh look, it has 'hope signs' on it."**

She had not meant to call them hope signs. But I loved it.

The symbol we have come to know as a symbol of peace is very much a sign of hope. It is meant to represent the foot of the dove, another symbol of peace. It has always been a very powerful symbol for me.

One type of peace is an outward peace, or a global peace. People are fighting in armies and militias every day, in causes and campaigns all around the world. Maybe there is a religious issue at hand, a land dispute, an oppressive government.

Whatever the reason for conflict, each side believes they are right. As a result, blood of the "guilty" and "innocent" fill the streets. Gunmen open fire in schools full of children. Chaos reigns. It is beyond our control.

Thankfully, what is in our control is inner peace, the peace within us. This can be somewhat of an amorphous concept for us. We can't see it, taste it, or touch it. We don't know how to describe or define it.

For me, peace is a multi-layered concept, much like the petals of a lotus flower. Serenity, compassion, empathy, acceptance, tolerance, and love are all found in peace.

Though bountiful, peace can be elusive. Sometimes it is found in tending a garden. In a moment of prayer. In meditation. Listening to your favorite music. Watching your favorite movie. Spending time with the ones you love. Relaxing in a bath. Reading a book.

The next time you see a peace symbol, a sign of hope, take a moment and pause.

How do you define peace?

Where do you find it?

No matter where you find it, how you define it, I hope you find peace today.

The world needs it.

And so do we.

# Equality

June 29, 2013

Last September I participated in the 100 Thousand Poets for Change, a global event to bring about positive change. I titled my submission "Change", which seemed apropos for the event. Here then is my poem, "Change."

There are many issues facing this world that I could have chosen to write about today-gun control in the United States, the effects of global warming, the children soldiers in Africa, war, genocide, hunger, poverty, literacy, racism, tolerance, coexistence, and more. All of these topics are valid and need a voice in the world, and need to be discussed. I have decided to talk about my views regarding a topic that is making headlines all over the world, which includes some of the previous categories. It is a civil rights issue, a global issue, and one that needs to be discussed. My topic of choice today is same sex marriage.

Many people have strong views on homosexuality, some religion-based, some fear based. I am not going to write anything here today that will change your mind about that issue. You have the right to your opinion, whether I share your opinion or not. However, if you are opposed to same sex marriage, I hope you will open your heart and mind just enough to listen to what
I have to say.

Regardless of your view on homosexuality, it must be understood that the issue of same sex marriage has nothing to do with religion. This is not a religious issue. This is a civil rights issue. The people of the world deserve to have their civil rights preserved, regardless of who they go to bed with. The rights of all citizens of the world need to be upheld, regardless of who someone decides to share their life with.

*Symphonies*

Around the world people are fighting for this basic human right every day. This is not just about standing in front of an altar and making a vow before God. There are many rights, benefits to marriage-financial, insurance benefits, even visiting people in hospitals that same sex couples are not afforded. People should have the right to marry whoever they want, whatever sex the person may be. Nothing should stand in the way of that-no person, no dogma, no politician, no government. You have every right to marry the person you love. Period. End of sentence. This is not and should not be a question of religion or politics. It is a question of rights. Basic, human, equal rights.

In the 1990s the U.S. created a law that stated that marriage is defined as between a man and a woman in the eyes of federal law. Because of this law, every homosexual marriage in the U.S. was denied the benefits, insurance coverage, financial benefits, and tax return standards afforded to all heterosexual marriages in the U.S. Immigration was also under this law as well; married people with spouses from other countries were not afforded the same immigration statuses or benefits. Many were in the process of being deported when the law was overturned. Service members in the U.S. military were affected as well; the law denied military members to acquire married housing, even to be notified upon the death of their spouse. In these ways and many others, this law was punitive and discriminatory against homosexuals in the United States.
It made every gay person in the U.S. a second class citizen.

Until this week. This past Wednesday, the U.S. Supreme Court found that law illegal because it discriminates Same-sex marriage is now federally recognized. Lives were instantly affected in the overturning of this law. I learned that the gay rights movement began 44 years ago in the United States. This verdict was a huge victory in the gay rights movement, and for

the country. Everyone should have equal rights.
Thomas Jefferson stated in his Declaration of Independence that "all men are created equal." ALL are created equal. Regardless of country of origin, gender, religious beliefs, sexual orientation. ALL are created EQUAL.

Last night in the state of California, wedding bells began to ring. Same-sex couples from across the country began to get married. Last night, on a cable news network,
I witnessed the wedding of a same-sex couple, plaintiffs in the case before the Supreme Court. Watching their wedding filled me with joy. It was very emotional, highly deserved and full of love. I will always remember that day, Wednesday, June 26, 2013. The day when my friends who are homosexual have the right to get married and have it recognized legally, by their state and by their country.

I am proud that my government has righted this wrong, that they have seen the level of discrimination in this law.
I am proud my country did the right thing. I am proud that we no longer discriminate against anyone, for any reason.
I am proud that we have equal rights for everyone. I am proud that the U.S. government believes in the words "all men are created equal", and that they are not just words on paper.

 Marriage equality has come to the U.S. It is here to stay.

I am a Christian, I am straight, and I am proud to be an American.

## Pursuit of Beauty                                       July 10, 2013

When you look in the mirror, what do you see? Your face? Your body? Your soul? What do you tell yourself about what you see?

Quite often I find that our inner voices come from a core of thoughts. The thoughts can protect us, yet can also hurt us. Women especially are very hard on themselves. Negative thoughts attack our self-esteem, self-image, self-worth, sense of power, sense of self.

4% of women around the world consider themselves beautiful. 80% of women know there is something beautiful about them, yet do not see the beauty within themselves. 90% of women would change at least one thing about their physical appearance.

There is no one form or vision of what is beautiful. There are as many ideals of beauty as there are countries in the world. What is idolized in one country is rejected in another.

Everyday women think and say things to themselves that we would never dream about saying to anyone else. Why then do women continue to say these things to themselves?

The pursuit of beauty, the quest for perfection, is doomed from the start. "Beauty is in the eye of the beholder." What may be beautiful to you may not be beautiful to me. But that does not mean that it does not exist. Beauty in its purest, truest form, lies within the soul.

It took me a while to come to the realization, or the differentiation, between my soul and my body. I have a body. Yet who I am as a person, the beauty that comes from within, from my soul, is separate from my body.

An interesting phenomenon has recently happened here in the United States-a campaign of body acceptance. Women are now being shown in advertisements that are above a size zero. Women are being reminded and told to value themselves, no matter their height, weight, and physical appearance.

Women have curves. We are meant to have curves. We have been created in this shape and form for a reason. The female form is divine.

Have you ever looked at the shape of the violin? A cello? A guitar? The bodies of these musical instruments were designed purposely and specifically in the shape of the curves of a woman's body, to immortalize the divinity of the female form. How has the pursuit of beauty surfaced in your life? How do you see others? How to you view the opposite sex? The same sex? What do you tell yourself about what you see? What judgments or assumptions have you made about others based solely on appearance? It is said that "beauty is only skin deep." The ugliest person can have the most beautiful soul, and vice versa.

I am more than my body. You are more than your body. We should not value ourselves because of our bodies. Our bodies are mere shells that our souls inhabit. I will not search for external beauty. I will only seek the true beauty that lies within. I will not define myself as a number on the scale. I am not my body. I am enough. I am beautiful.

*Symphonies*

## Misconceptions                    July 13, 2013

A misconception is defined as a mistaken idea or notion.
I heard a very interesting question the other day-
"What misconceptions do people have about you?" The immediate answer in my head was, "Plenty!" I think there are many misconceptions that surround us all. I thought
I would go over a few of the answers I came up with in my mind.

The first misconception about me is that I do not speak English. My name as it is seen here is my pen name, not my real name. I chose this name because, in Spanish, it means "Hope Speaks." I think hope should speak; it truly has a lot to say. I learned a humorous fact about my pen name the other day; I was told by an online friend that it means "Stupid Car" in their language. Go figure. ;)

When people see my name, whether online, in an e-mail, in a social network, on this blog, people tend to think I am of Latin descent, either from Spain or South America, and that I am learning English. In fact, it is the opposite. I am an American citizen, born and raised; English is my native tongue, and I am learning Spanish.

I have been learning Spanish for three years now. I have found that, even at work, people will come in and be surprised that I know Spanish. I understand it; to look at me, you would not think that I know a word of Spanish.

I find it amusing when I hear adults talking to their children and they say, **"Tell her that…"** in Spanish. I listen to try and find out what the problem is. I then say, "Oh, do you speak Spanish?" in Spanish. Quite often the reaction is stunned silence, with a nodding of the head. At that point

I converse with them and find out how I can help them.

On another topic, many misconceptions have arisen in my life because I am single. There are many questions, even stigmas that accompany this status. I hear many statements, such as:

> *"You must be so lonely, living all alone."*
> *"So where is Mr. Right?"*
> *"Do you not want to get married?"*
> *"You actually go places by yourself?!?"*
> *"How are you going to have any children if you don't meet a man?"*
> *"How are you going to meet a man if you're not looking?"*
> *"There must be something wrong with you if you are in your 40's and have never been married."*
> *"What do you mean you don't want children?"*

I have heard so many of these statements in my life that at this point, frankly, I find them amusing. Truth be told, I do not live alone. I share my space with two adorable kittens. In terms of human cohabitants, yes, I live alone. I prefer it that way.
I bought my own home over ten years ago now. After the experience of having roommates in college, I was bound and determined to not have a roommate again.

I love the personal freedom that living alone brings me.
I love having my own space, not having to share it with anyone, watching what I want to watch on TV when I want to watch it. As far as love and romance are concerned, of course I would love to get married. But only in the instance of a true love, a forever love. Maybe that is still in the cards for me. Maybe not. I am not actively looking for love. However, if love finds me, that would be just fine. As far as children are

concerned, I do not want children. I grew up knowing I never wanted to have children. I never got along with children even when I was one. I do not want children. If I fall in love and the man wants children, well, we're going to have to talk about that. But let it be known-I do not need a man in my life or children to be happy.

Lastly, I think the most misconceptions arise in my life because I am overweight. Others use words like "fat" or "morbidly obese." Of the words listed here, I am most comfortable with "overweight." When people think of the word "fat", it brings up many images, many misconceptions:

*"Fat people are lazy."*
*"Fat people smell."*
*"Fat people binge eat."*
*"Fat people are unhealthy."*
*"Fat people eat twice the amount food
than normal people do."*
*"I'd rather die than be fat."*

I feel the word "fat" is derogatory. I do not equate anyone with the word "fat."

Thoughts are one thing; comments that are misconceptions, regarding me, and my body, are another. Comments can range from quiet concern to blatant abuse...

**"You would be so pretty if you lost weight."**
**"Wow, she has really let herself go."**
**"What happened to you?!?"**
**"Are you sure you want to eat that?
That has so many calories in it."**
**"Don't take this the wrong way, but, my church
has a weight loss prayer group this weekend.
We would love to have you."**

> "Wow, you remember that? I guess it is true-elephants never do forget."
> "Look at her legs-they look like ham hocks. She should be hanging in a butcher shop window."

There have been many similar comments, from which I will spare you. If someone makes a comment about me, about my weight, whether in gentle concern or disdain, that comment is not going to magically change my body type.

There are many types of people-those who eat and eat and never gain an ounce; those that gain weight after eating an apple. This can be explained quite easily. Scientists have recently discovered the "fat gene", called "Plin2". In people who are overweight, this gene processes fats and sugars differently.

People are not overweight because they are lazy-their body processes foods differently. It is simple genetics. Some hope that, knowing the "Plin2" gene has been discovered, testing can be done to "turn off" this gene, and help people lose weight. I might try that. I would love to eat a cookie and not gain an ounce.

When all is said and done, misconceptions are just as the definition states-a mistaken idea or notion. They are rampant in our world; they can range from innocent to inciting. They can be general, global, and highly personal.

What are your misconceptions? What do you think or say about others? What do others mistakenly think about you?

*Symphonies*

# Glorious Sky                          July 18, 2013

I wander through the moment looking down, watching my feet as I walk. Something within me shifts. I feel guided from above. *"Look up you fool! You are missing it! Look up!!!!"*
I hear a voice say. I do as I am guided. I look up.

 There before my eyes, the most wondrous sky I have ever seen. Such a vivid hue of cobalt blue. A sky so blue you could get lost in it. The sky is truly amazing. It looks animated. No, not animated. Painted. It is clear the great artist used the most vibrant blue in their palette. Three dimensional whimsical white clouds dot the skyscape, completing the scene.

I would love to sit in the grass, lay in the grass, and look at the sky, watch the sky go by, and lose myself in that glorious sky.

*Avebury, England, 1997 by Esperanza Habla*

# The Mask of the Moon          July 23, 2013

Last night, upon gazing out my window, I saw the full moon, the Thunder Moon, light up the nighttime sky with an amber hue. As the sky around it darkened, the moon shone in her true beauty.

I immediately reached for my camera. The first few images I took were out of focus, blurry, not at all showing the true brilliance I saw before my eyes. I later got some very nice photos, in sharp focus, with great detail.

I then left that window, and went to another. I lifted the camera to my eye. At that moment, I saw a double image of the moon. I took a photo. The double image I had seen showed up in the photograph. I questioned my eyesight and shut my eyes to give them a momentary rest. I opened them again, and still saw a double image of the moon.

I suppose the double image can be explained because I was taking the photo through a window, through a pane of glass, not as my eye would naturally see it while looking at the sky outside. But there on my camera was the double image of the moon, just as my eye had seen it.

The photo could be seen as an error, because I took the photo from behind a pane of glass. I do not see it that way at all. I see it as a stroke of luck, an uncommon occurrence; my friend Luna was letting me see a side of herself that I had never been privileged to see, a way that I had never seen her before.

In the photograph, the image we normally see when we look at a full moon, the "face" of the moon, is on the left; on the right,

the moon, an amber orb of light, shining in all of her glory.

*Symphonies*

To me, it looks as if the "face" of the moon is really the mask of the moon-the face the moon shows to everyone in the universe. I was lucky enough to have captured Luna taking off her mask, showing her true, abundant self, the essence of her being.

Thank you Luna, for taking off your mask, letting me see the beauty of who you really are.

*"The Mask of the Moon" by Esperanza Habla*

*Symphonies*

## It Was Fifty Years Ago Today     July 25, 2013

Today, while watching a morning news program/talk show, I found out that 2013 is the 50 year mark of the music group the Beatles. Their first album was released in March of 1963.

I was shocked and surprised when I heard this fact. I am in my early 40s. The group was formed and had broken up before I was born. I wrote a poem about how I first found out about the Beatles, entitled, "Where were You?"

I was eight years old when John Lennon died. His death began my search for knowledge on the Beatles. I would later learn their names: John Lennon, Paul McCartney, George Harrison, Ringo Starr.

I once heard a quote that said the Beatles music in our D.N.A. If you are a fan of the Beatles music, I would agree with that statement. Their music has such an iconic sound. If you hear the inner chords to any of their famous, chart topping songs, you immediately know what group is playing and what the song is.

For years I have wondered what it is about the Beatles music that made them the most popular band on the planet. Was it the music and lyrics of Lennon and McCartney? Was it their writing style? Was it a unique sound they created? Was it their message of peace and love? Was it the four individuals coming together to make music? Was it their unique voices in harmony? Was it their own, individual, unique talents? Was it a clever marketing campaign? Was it because they created the music video? (Actually, the very first music videos were made as short films to accompany songs. The first band to ever do this was the Beatles.) Whatever it was that set them apart, made them different, it changed the music industry, film, the world forever.

## *Symphonies*

A friend of mine recently had the extreme good fortune of seeing Sir Paul McCartney live on his latest tour. I would have loved to have seen him. I do not have a "bucket list" (a list of things I want to do before I die); however, if I did have such a list, seeing McCartney live would be on it. The closest I have come to any of the Beatles was on the Everyone Matters website. Everyone Matters is a campaign to promote tolerance and acceptance of others. They have many celebrities that act as spokespeople for the cause. One of the celebrities is Sir Paul McCartney. In October of last year, Everyone Matters featured me and my work. There was a story about me on Facebook, which was also shown on the Everyone Matters page. So for a day, I was on the same website as Sir Paul McCartney.
I remember calling my mother, shouting:
**"I'm on the same web page as a BEATLE!"**
     http://everyone-matters.com/

Their music has been used in movies, referenced in movies and pop culture; movies have been created about the Beatles, and their music. There is even a Cirque du Soleil show in Las Vegas that is a Beatles music experience. The characters of their songs are represented by actors on the stage. (Seeing that show would be on a list of things I would love to do before I die as well.)

If you were to ask me if the Beatles music is in my DNA, I am not sure of my answer. I was not alive when the band was formed, or when they broke up. I do not know every song they have ever done; I do not know all the words. I do not know all the trivia about the Beatles, or about the men in the group. That being said, I am definitely a fan of their music. I know many of their songs, many of the words. I have a poster in my home that shows every Beatles album cover, with every song listed.

The Beatles were and are a global phenomenon. In the days before the internet, before social media, before YouTube, their music reached around the world, across barriers of cultures and languages. To this day their music is part of a global lexicon. Their music transcends time and space. In recent history, four mini planets, were found in space. They were named John, Paul, George Ringo. Their music literally resounds across the universe.

# A Grateful Heart    July 26, 2013

When I began my writing career three years ago, I had no idea what the future would bring. My friends A, C, L and S suggested I write, to express what I was thinking and feeling. I shared my first poems with them; they were positive in their comments, and encouraged me to write more. The more I wrote, the more I looked forward to sharing my poems with my friends. They supported me and my writing, and encouraged me to continue.

Months after I began writing, my confidence had grown. One day I asked a friend what he thought about my creating a blog of my writing. He encouraged me to create a blog. With much trepidation, I built my first blog, "Words of Hope." At first, the blog was private-I only let A, C, L and S read what I had written. I was not confident in my skills as a writer. I did not have the courage to share my writing with anyone else.

## Symphonies

I then had a discussion with my friend L. He asked when I was going to make the blog public. I told him I did not know; I did not feel ready for that. He then said, "What if you could help someone with your writing? What if you could help someone who is going through a similar issue, or hard time in their life?" L was right. I immediately went to the blog and changed the settings to public.

Over the years I continued to write on my blog, in Spanish and English. My blog became more and more popular, and I became more confident as a writer. Then the folks here at Blogger created a new feature on their pages, "Translate." I thought that would be a better idea for me, for me to post my poems in English, and then have the website translate the poem for the reader, in their language. I then decided to create a new blog, this blog, "Letters to the Moon."

In December of 2012 I let my readers know that I was going to be changing blogs with the New Year, and my reasoning for doing so. I shared the link to this blog, so my readers could find me. On my first blog, I averaged 20-30 people a month. I was happy with those numbers; I hoped that people would follow me to my new blog. They followed me alright.

This blog is the most successful thing I have ever done. Since its launch, I have had over 10,000 visitors, from more than 30 countries around the world, including the United States, Peru, Russia, France, Mexico, Germany, Argentina, Colombia, Australia, the Netherlands, Japan, Serbia, Albania, India, Thailand and more. Blog visits average more than 1,200 a month.

When I began writing, I never dreamed that I would start a blog, let alone two. I never dreamed that readers around the globe would be reading my poetry. I never dreamed that readers would have the opportunity to read my words and thoughts in their language. As I opened up my heart and began to write, so did the world.

The journey is just beginning. I have created my own publishing company, La Luna Press, to publish collections of my poetry. I will have two volumes poetry, called "I am Hope" and "The Bigger Picture", which will be available in Spanish and English. My hope is to have the books ready for purchase by 2014. I am also working on my first novel, "Samantha", which I hope to have ready by 2015.

I want to thank my family for their continued support, and for helping me to realize my dream. I want to thank my friends A, C, L, S, who first encouraged me to write. I want to thank my friends A, A, X, B, R, M, who continue to sustain me.

I also want to thank all of the artists I have met around the world, of all art forms, for your friendship, for welcoming me as a fellow artist, for your unwavering support of me and my writing. Thank you especially to C, E, M, E, P, J, D, L, N, E. Your support and friendship mean so much to me. I also want to thank Candice Terry for featuring me as the author day on her blog, and to Everyone Matters for featuring me.

Finally, I want to thank you, the reader, for continuing to read my work. I promise I will continue to write as inspiration comes. Thank you for your continued support. Thank you for reading the words of hope, and the letters to the moon. The support you have shown me means more than you will ever know. I truly write this to you with a humble, thankful, and grateful heart.

*Symphonies*

## The Meaning of Life                      July 1, 2013

for eons people have questioned the meaning of life.

*"What is the meaning of life? What are we here for? What is my purpose?"*

Perhaps the meaning of life is to create art-to engage in the world around us, to absorb all we can about the world around us, and translate it into art.

Maybe the meaning of life is to love-to love and be loved in every meaning of the word, to love your spouse, significant other, family, friends and never take them for granted.

Perhaps the meaning of life is different for every person. Maybe each of us has our own, unique meaning of life, unique to our realities and circumstances.

I feel I have found the meaning of life, as well as my purpose.

Over the last three years I have realized something that was within me all along, something I never knew existed-the talent for writing. When I began writing, my friends told me that my writing was good, and encouraged me to continue. I did not believe that I had any talent as a writer; I thought my friends were just being nice to me. To my surprise, my friends were being truly honest with me. They genuinely thought I had talent as a writer and encouraged me to continue to write.

When I began my first blog, the Words of Hope, it was a private blog. It was only open to those I invited to the site. My confidence in my writing was growing, but I was not fully confident as a poet and artist. A friend and fellow author encouraged me to make the blog public. I was very hesitant to opening up the blog for everyone in the world to read. Then my friend said the words, "What if you can help someone? What if reading your writing could help someone with something they are going through, or struggling with? What if you could help someone?" Those words instantly changed my mind, and I made the blog visible to everyone.

About a year ago, those words came true. I had two online friends who were going through a struggle in their lives. They came to me to talk about what they were feeling and going through. I then sent them something I had written, hoping it might help. To my shock, it did help them. They were thankful I had shared my writings and commented about how much better they felt. Someone else knew what they were feeling, what they were going through. They were not alone.

To my total surprise and delight, my friend's comments had come true. I cannot tell you what a gift that was, to know that I actually helped someone. Something I had written made a difference in someone's life. It was a profoundly humbling, powerful moment.

I feel that is my purpose in life, to write about my experiences, to share my thoughts and feelings, through poem and verse.
I feel that that is the true meaning of life for us all-to find your talents and use them to help as many people as you possibly can.

I believe we are given our talents for a reason. We may not know the reason; we may not know we have the talent. My writing is the best way I can fulfill, find, and perhaps complete the meaning of life.

Find your talents and use them to help as many people as you can.

*Symphonies*

*"Hide not your talents, they for use were made."*
*-Benjamin Franklin*

*"The meaning of life is to find your gift.*
*The purpose in life is to give it away."*
*-Pablo Picasso*

*"According to this law [the law of Dharma],*
*you have a unique talent*
*and a unique way of expressing it.*
*There is something that you can do*
*better than anyone else in the whole world—*
*and for every unique talent*
*and unique expression of that talent,*
*there are also unique needs.*
*When these needs are matched*
*with the creative expression of your talent,*
*that is the spark that creates affluence.*
*Expressing your talents to fulfill needs creates*
*unlimited wealth and abundance."*
*— Deepak Chopra*

# The Act of Comparison         August 6, 2013

Writers thrive on inspiration. Sometimes we find inspiration, and sometimes, as in this case, inspiration finds us. Yesterday I had an idea in my head for a poem. After some thought, I decided it was way too personal a subject to write about. However, over the course of my day many quotes, images, thoughts on the subject crossed my path. It was as if I was meant to see these things to change my mind. After more reflection, I discovered the topic in question is a universal issue. I could not ignore the signs.
I knew I had to write about it.

  I have noticed something, with my new eye on the world, which can have both positive and negative effects. I am referring to the act of comparison. These days, many comparisons are made in entertainment news. Critics will compare a new, up and coming singer to a seasoned singer. Journalists will compare a new film maker's style to that of an accomplished film maker. People compare a new fashion line to one of a famous designer. Reviewers will say the writing style of one author is reminiscent of another. Those types of comparisons are benign and are beneficial to an artist.

  However, there are other types of comparisons that we make, in our relationships with others, towards other people. At any given time we can have an internal monologue in our head, with thoughts such as:

> *"I love her hair. I wish my hair would hold a curl like that."*

> *"Her skin is flawless. I would love to have her complexion."*

> *"Look at that new car he is driving.*
> *You can tell he is making money.*
> *I would love to have a car like that."*

> *"This house is amazing. This is my dream house.*
> *I have always wanted to live in a house like this."*

> *"Wow-she is phenomenal.*
> *Is there anything she cannot do?"*

Comparisons can become darker, more destructive from there. In my writing career, I have been fortunate to meet artists all around the world. I have found that, many times, people are more than their profession. For example, I work in a library; in addition, I also write on this blog, and have formed my own publishing company.

Some more examples: I know an artist who teaches and is also a musician. I have met a poet who also performs ballet. I even have one online friend who is an actor, dancer, model, clown, mime, aerialist, musician, poet, playwright, teacher, and puppeteer.

To hear of someone who has so many talents, you might think,
**"Wow! What a talented individual!"**

Or, you might think,
**"Wow. And all I can do is knit a scarf."**

Comparisons are not bad things in and of themselves. However, they should be treated with caution. Making comparisons can make us feel bad about ourselves and ruin our self-esteem. Sometimes we do this without even realizing we are doing it. When we make negative comparisons, we are sabotaging ourselves. We are negating our talents, our gifts, our blessings, and everything we have been given.

Theodore Roosevelt once said that "Comparison is the thief joy."

Iyanla Vanzant, minister and spiritual leader, has a more direct quote:
> ***"Comparison is an act of violence against the self."***

If you notice that you have made a comparison which made you feel bad about yourself, release the comparison.

You were given an abundance of gifts, an abundance of talents, an abundance of riches, and an abundance of blessings. Everything that was given to you was given to you for a reason.

You are a shining light. Let your light shine. You never know what dark corners of the universe your light will illuminate.

*Symphonies*

## It Was Not My Time                August 7, 2013

I have been thinking of an incident from my past. I do not know why I have been thinking about it lately. It is not the anniversary of the event, it has no bearing on my life now, or how I life my life. Yet, the memory is there, and it continues. Maybe I am supposed to write about it.

What you are about to read actually happened to me. 100% of it is true.

I can remember at ten years of age going away on summer vacation and visiting relatives that lived out of my state.
It was nice to visit these relatives; we only got to see them maybe once a year.

I do not remember the city they lived in, I barely remember their apartment. There is one thing I do remember about that visit and my surroundings-the pool.

Like many apartment complexes, it had a pool. I remember going there one day on my visit with one of my relatives.
I went into the pool, played, and had a good time. I had been taking swimming lessons, so I knew how to orient myself by touching my feet to the bottom of the pool.

I could do a few swimming strokes, and knew basic swimming techniques. In my swimming classes, I was in an indoor swimming pool that was all the same depth. I had had some experience in swimming in the deeper end of a pool, but not much. I knew to stay close to the edge of the pool in the deep end; I could not touch my feet to the bottom of the pool, but I could grab the side of the pool if I needed help or orientation.

A few minutes had passed, though I cannot remember how many. It could have been ten minutes, it could have been thirty. Suddenly, a little girl swam up to me. She said I was a great swimmer; I thanked her for the compliment. She asked if I could take her to the deep end of the pool. She really wanted to go to the deeper end, though I had no idea why.

I remember feeling hesitant when she asked me. I did not understand why she needed my help to get to the deeper end of the pool, which was less than five feet away from her. But, I knew I had some confidence in my swimming, and I thought I could handle it. Ignoring my instincts, I said yes. I should have listened to my instincts.

I took her arm and we began to swim into the deeper end of the pool. As we got closer, she moved closer to me. She held on to me, sort of in a loose embrace. I stayed close to the edge like I was comfortable with.

**"No, I want to go out into the middle,"** she told me.

I rolled my eyes in frustration, kicked off from the side of the pool and went towards the middle of the deep end. That is when the panic set in. Not in me, but in my swimming companion.

I then knew why the little girl needed my help to get to the deeper end of the pool; she could not swim. She could keep her head above water, but could do very little else.

She had no business being in the pool to begin with. And quite frankly, I should never have said yes to her request to take her into the deeper end of the pool.

## *Symphonies*

The little girl began to panic. There we were, in the middle of the deep end. She began to hold on to me more closely, tightening her grip around me. That is when I began to panic. I reached for the bottom of the pool with my feet.

I of course could not reach it; we were now in the deep end of the pool. The pool depth could have been eight feet deep; it could have been twenty feet deep for all I knew.

I tried to calm the girl, telling her it was alright, and that I would get her to the other side. That is when she had a panic attack.

She used me to get herself higher in the water, which meant I was being pushed down into the water.

I struggled to the surface and took a quick breath. Again the girl pushed me down into the water.

I remember looking up as I was going down into the water. I remember seeing a woman, in a bikini style swimsuit, jump in after us. Actually, in my memory, I see her in sort of a "Matrix" movie moment, suspended in midair, frozen in a second in time.

The next thing I knew, I was in a dark place. I was nowhere, yet I was somewhere. I could breathe. I was no longer in the water. I was in sort of a large room; it had light, yet the walls and floor were black. I remember looking up, to my left, and seeing a large, rectangular object, similar to a movie screen. At first, the screen was lit up with white light.

Suddenly, a movie began; it was the movie of my life. I watched my life flash in front of my eyes. Images from my life, my memories, flashed in front of my eyes, moving faster than I could fathom. Occasionally, an image would pause, if only for a fraction of a second. The film then sped up again to normal speed. I watched those images. I remember seeing these images.

I then received a message. It did not come to me in an audible voice; no one said it to me. It did not come in a yell or a whisper. The message came to me in a thought. I do not know how I received this message. Yet I received it all the same:

IT IS NOT YOUR TIME.

The next thing I knew, I was out of the water, sitting in a chair on the pool desk, a warm towel wrapped around me.
I have no idea how I got from the water to that chair. I was scared and confused. I have no memory of what happened after I went down in the water the second time.

A moment later, the little girl, who had asked me to take her to the deep end of the pool, walked up to me. She was also wrapped in a towel. She apologized to me. I nodded my head in response. I remember thinking,

*"Yeah yeah, it's okay. Get away from me."*

She walked away. I then heard in the distance,
**"Hey, can you take me to the deep end?"**
It was the same little girl, asking someone else.

Looking back on the incident, I do not remember being in a tunnel. I do not remember seeing a white light. I was not met by a deceased family member. I was alone in that dark place, watching my life flash before my eyes. I was someplace else; and then, in an instant, I was not.

## *Symphonies*

You might read this and think I had a near death experience. You may read this and think I passed out due to lack of oxygen to my brain. You might think that I made this up and have a vivid imagination. As I said in the beginning, this story happened to me, and is 100% true.

This event has not had a large impact on my life. I still swim, I am not afraid of the water. I do not have any fear of water. I swim in the shallow and deep ends of a pool.

I do not know if the woman in the bikini got me out of the water. I do not know if she saved me, or if someone else did. I do know, however, that a higher power was involved.

However it happened, however I was saved, I want to give my universal thanks to anyone and everyone involved in saving me.

I knew I was saved for a reason.

I knew that I was saved for a purpose.

I knew that it was not my time.

*Symphonies*

# Visible                                  August 9, 2013

Through my becoming a poet, creating a blog, branching out in social media, I have become friends with many people throughout the world. I love that I have the opportunity to meet so many people, from different places on the planet. These are people I have not met in person, but would never have had the chance to meet at all were it not for the internet. Many are artists; they represent many forms of art, including the art of mime. Mime is not an art form that is generally seen in the United States. My first introduction to mime was as a child, watching Robert Shields and Lorene Yarnell perform on the Muppet Show. I was maybe seven, eight years old. I have admired the art form ever since.

About a year ago, I was on one of my favorite sites, Pinterest. I saw a photo of a mime artist, on a page called the Silence Community; I clicked "like" on the photo, and continued to look at other photos on the site. A day or two later, I received a message from a gentleman in France. He wrote me and introduced himself; he said that he is a mime, and that he had created a social network called the Silence Community. He said that the network was for performers who perform dance, physical theater, mime, and gestural theater; he then went on to say that the community is also open to people who are not performers, yet love and or admire those forms of art. He gave me the link to the website, and said I was more than welcome in the community. I joined the very same day.

The Silence Community is a social network, much like Facebook, in which members can friend one another, post videos, create groups, have discussions. When I joined I filled out my profile with my information, my blog address, and that I am a poet, writer, and translator. Through making new friends on the site, I found out that my talents might be of use to the Silence Community. I was asked by the same gentleman, the founder of the site, to translate some of the items on the website, from English to Spanish. The community has over 200 members, with members around the world. The network has many languages to accommodate every member.

Over the last year, having conversations with this gentleman and others, I have grown in my role in the Silence Community. For a period of time this year, from March until May, I served as the web administrator for the community. It is unique in that it is completely funded by donations from its members. It costs over 700 euros, close to $1,000 U.S. dollars, to run every year. A little over a week ago, the founder of the Silence Community created a Facebook page for the community, to let others know of its existence, and to encourage more people to join. I have been appointed the administrator of the Facebook page. For my translation work and web administration with the Silence Community, the administration of the Facebook page, and for my monetary donation, I received the honor of being appointed to the Board of Directors in the Silence Community.

Perhaps the most famous mime in the world was Marcel Marceau. I got to see him perform in one of his tours to the U.S. in the 1990s. He passed away in 2007. One of the things he said about the art of mime was that the goal of the art form was to "make the invisible visible." Mime is a simple and yet very complex art form at the same time. Mimes are trained to tell complete stories with their body. The training is very demanding and intense. One exercise students are given is to tell a story through the use of one body part, like a hand, leg, or a foot. Could you tell a story without words, using only your foot?

You may be reading this and thinking to yourself, "You are a writer. What does writing have to do with mime?" While learning the complexities of art of mime, it occurred to me that mimes and writers do exactly the same thing: they tell a story. Everything we create comes from nothing. We make the invisible visible.

Both writers and mimes convey thoughts, feelings, and stories through storytelling. The mime uses their body movements in actions to convey the story, to show you what cannot be seen; the writer uses their words, in descriptive narrative, to tell the story, and to show you what cannot be seen.

Poetry is the art of words; mime is the poetry of the body.

I have a new found respect for the art of mime and for the art of writing. Realizing my role as a writer makes me approach my writing more seriously. I now know that I have a big job to do; I have to help everyone see what they cannot.

I must make the invisible visible.

If you are interested in joining the Silence Community, here are the links:

Silence Community:

www.silencecommunity.com

Silence Community Facebook Page:

www.facebook.com/silencecommunity.page

## Symphonies

Friendship, Love, Sex, Truth, Lies, Hope, Hate, and the Internet
August 16, 2013

The internet and the worldwide web have opened up new worlds for everyone that has internet access. It has opened up new possibilities for countless millions. But is everything possible? When considering friendship, love, sex, the truth, lies, hope, hate, is everything possible on the internet?

Many have asked about me about my online _friendships_. "Are you really friends with these people?" I can tell you that I have made friends through social media. Over time, some of my online contacts have truly become close friends. Some I talk with occasionally; some I talk to more frequently than my friends who live five minutes away. Some of my friends offer hugs and kisses from afar; some even say "I Love You." Is a genuine friendship on the internet possible? Absolutely.

_Love_-now there is a topic. Is love possible on the internet? Ask the countless thousands who have found a mate online. Every day I see a commercial for a dating website on the internet. They have dating websites now that cater to specific demographics-Christians, people of a certain age, people of specific ethnicities, even farmers! I have a dear friend who has used online dating cites, and has found a great match. Connections can be made everywhere, even online.

Is it possible to fall in love on the internet? Yes. I have a friend who dated a man online. They spoke many times a day, through social media and personal e-mail. They had a friendship that lasted years; over the course of their relationship, their friendship turned into love. She had very little contact with this individual in person; they lived about 100 miles apart from one another. The majority of their time together was online. Their love grew, and they were engaged to be married. Unfortunately, their relationship did not last. Yes love is possible. Even on the internet. Love is everywhere.

That of course leads us to the topic of <u>sex</u> on the internet. People go online for pornography, to meet people online, to find a group or person to fulfill their need. Some go with good intentions; others end up committing adultery. In addition, there is a current trend in the U.S. in which young men, in their teen and college years, solicit young women for sex, through text messages and e-mail. Young men think that this is how to meet women. Young women think that accepting these advances from young men is the way to get the young man to like her. We are in what is called a "super sexualized culture." It is in our movies, television, media. It is no wonder that these young men think this is an acceptable way to meet women.

Now let me tell you something that actually happened, to me. One night I was chatting with one of my online friends. During the course of our conversation, this friend tried to initiate cyber-sex with me. I had never been flirtatious with him and I did not have feelings for him. His trying to initiate cyber-sex with me made me quite uncomfortable.

I instantly ended the conversation, and the friendship. I thought he was being friendly with me; in reality, he was being flirtatious. Even though we were thousands of miles away from one another, he was looking for one thing from me; I however was not.

This naturally then brings us to the topic of the <u>truth and lies</u>. I was told once that "everyone lies." The person that told me that turned out to be a pathological liar. However, in some ways, I believe that is true. We often lie to one another to protect someone's feelings. However, there is a growing trend online to pretend you are someone you are not. People load a photo online, pose as that person, and manipulate people into believing that is who they are. Sexual predators have done this online for years. But simpler, less devastating lies happen online all the time. People pretend to be something they are not. People tell you they are single when they are in fact married. We tell people we feel one thing when we feel another. People tell you they love you when in fact they feel nothing of the sort.

Is _hope_ possible on the internet? Undeniably. There are many initiatives and causes on the internet that cannot but fill a person with hope. Pages on every social media entity are filled with uplifting images of positivity, peace and hope. I have seen countless examples of hope on the internet. Do not doubt it.

Is _hate_ possible on the internet? Like love, hate seems to be everywhere. Since the invention of the internet, hate has had a place on it. Lately, hate has found a home in social media. Anyone can hide behind a profile photo, post a comment and create a feeling of negativity. This negativity can also be construed as hate.

I recently wrote a piece that discussed the topic of racism in America. When I had finished writing the piece, I shared it on Facebook and Twitter and Google+, as I always do. After posting the above piece, I saw numerous comments to the post. The piece definitely struck a nerve.

Several people posted comments, which later resulted in them being verbally attacked for their point of view. As I continued to read, I saw that I myself was under attack. Some comments questioned me, my point of view, my motives for writing such a piece, for sharing the piece, and even my level of intellect. Every other comment was filled with hatred. I deleted the post immediately. I do not mind if someone does not share my opinion; however I will not be a party to negativity and hatred.

Slain civil rights leader Medgar Evers once said:
> ***"Hate is a wasteful emotion,***
> ***most of the people you hate***
> ***don't know you hate them***
> ***and the rest don't care."***

Hate is a weapon that should never be aimed at anyone. Hate is a parasite; much like a tick, it has to have a host to survive. I refuse to be a host to such a parasite.

The internet is a wonderful tool. It can bring us employment, give us learning opportunities; it can be showcase for art, can be a place of personal growth It is also a home for friendship, love, sex, truth, lies, hope, and hate. Anything and everything under the moon can be found on the internet. Sometimes we go seeking these things; sometimes, these things find us.
I choose to seek out friendship, and the truth. What do you seek out?

> ***"I have decided to stick with love.***
> ***Hate is too great a burden to bear."***
> ***-Martin Luther King Jr.***

*Symphonies*

# I Know  August 20, 2013

*A letter to a friend

I know what it feels like, to be let down by someone. I know this must be very painful you, because the person who let you down is a family member. I know how it feels to pray for a person, that they would be who they used to be, who they need to be. I know how it feels, when reality sets in, when the truth settles, and you realize that your prayers were not answered in the way you wanted them to be.

I know how it feels to realize that that person cannot be what you want them-or need them-to be. I know the pain of letting go of those hopes and expectations. I know how it feels to step back from the situation, and step out of their toxicity. I also know that prayer does work. I know that life, sometimes painfully, goes on. I know that I cannot fix anyone.

I know that everyone on Earth matters, and that we are all here to have experiences and to learn from them. I hope that person will learn everything they are here to learn.
I know that we need to take care of ourselves, love ourselves, learn from the situation, do what is necessary to keep ourselves whole, and distance ourselves from negativity.
I know that talking helps, along with prayer, reflection, writing, as well as shopping and chocolate.

What I want you to know is that I am here for you, however you need me to be.

## Another Day is Done             August 22, 2013

I return from a day at work filled with chaos; our busiest day in months. I feel nothing but stress and exhaustion.

I climb the stairs to my home, turn the key, let myself in, lock the door behind me and lean my back against it, sighing in relief. I am finally home. Another day is done.

I am met by my two kittens; they are glad to see that mama is home. I pet each of the kittens. They relish the affection. One of the kittens jumps to reach my hand.

She reminds me of a horse that stands up on its hind legs and bucks. She is my bucking bronco. I fill their food bowl with a scoop of food. The kittens eat and purr contentedly.

I prepare my evening meal, and then sit on the couch.
I turn on the television to the national news. I soon have a kitten on the couch with me. She is content to keep my company, yet wants to help me finish my meal.

I continue watching the news. The kitten has now moved closer. She has settled down, lying against my legs.

Soon after, my other kitten comes for a visit; she jumps up and rests on the arm of the couch. She then decides to come lay on me, on top of my chest. It is her favorite spot; she loves to lay on top of me, to feel my heartbeat, to feel my chest raise and fall with my breath.

All is quiet and still. There is no sound in the room but the television. Daylight is leaving, night is coming. I lay on the couch with one kitten next to me, the other kitten on top of me.

## *Symphonies*

Soon another friend comes to visit. I look to the window; the curtains are parted. There before my eyes, my friend the moon.

I feel a sense of relief, seeing my friend. I talk to my friend Luna in thoughts and whispers. The kitten on my chest turns to me, as if asking what I said.

I tell her I am talking to my friend Luna. The kitten looks out the window, noticing my friend. She then lays her head down again, in quiet contentment.

A peaceful time, surrounded by purring, enveloped by the warmth of the kittens, bathed in moonlight.

My kitties and my eternal best friend are with me.

I sink into the couch, in total relaxation and peace after a day of chaos.

Another day is done.

# Alike                              August 24, 2013

Next month I am participating in the One Hundred Thousand Poets for Change event. I took part in this event last year, which had a great success around the world. There are many things I could write about for that topic.

I think I have found a topic to write about. But for now, there is a topic that I would like to discuss now. It is relevant, and needs discussing. The following writing has videos and photos to accompany the topic. Please read and watch with an open mind and an open heart.

There is one topic on the mind of many Americans right now; that topic is race. Earlier this year, the Supreme Court of the U.S. repealed a voting rights act that was written into law in the 1960s. Many people fought and died for the right for all to vote, regardless of color.

The ruling from the Supreme Court was a huge step backwards in equal rights in the U.S. The court ruled this way because the court feels that we live in a "post-racist" society, meaning, in their minds, that racism does not exist in anymore. As anyone can tell the court, racism does exist. It exists all around the world.

To be clear, racism is defined as: the belief that all members of each race possess characteristics or abilities specific to that race, esp. so as to distinguish it as inferior or superior to another race or races. (Google definition)

Fifty years ago, on August 28, 1963, there was a march on Washington, made famous by the "I Have a Dream" speech by Martin Luther King Jr. It was originally planned to be a march for jobs and freedom. It became a march for equality, the defining moment in the civil rights movement in the United States.

Today in Washington D.C., there is another march on Washington, to commemorate the event fifty years ago. The U.S. has come a long way in those fifty years. But we have a long way to go.

There are many other words that accompany racism. One I learned recently, is called colorism. Colorism is defined as: **a practice of discrimination by which those with lighter skin are treated more favorably than those with darker skin.** (About.com definition)

I knew that such discrimination existed; I learned of the existence of colorsim from the controversial movie, "Imitation of Life."

More recently, I watched a documentary called "Dark Girls", which discusses colorism. The documentary was fascinating to watch. I learned many things I never knew before. I learned that colorism is found in the black culture, the Latino culture, and other cultures around the world.

Another word that goes along with racism is the word bias. This word can be defined as: cause to feel or show inclination or prejudice for or against someone or something. (Google definition.)

Biases border on the subconscious and stereotypes based on things that are not true. They are often shown in ways we are not always aware of. In a recent racial bias test from Harvard University, 70% of the white people who took the test had racial biases, and of black people who took the test, 45% had racial biases.

*Symphonies*

In a recent advertisement on television, a family was shown, made up of a white mother, a black father, and biracial child. Many adults protested the commercial, for showing a family of mixed races. Many people just saw the commercial, and did not notice the color of the actors. Interracial families exist; they should be represented on television.

I have heard people say, **"living in an urban setting made me a racist"** and say **"that is just how I was raised."** All of us have racial beliefs and biases, to some extent, whether we are aware of them or not. This does not mean that we would act violently towards someone of another race, or join the hate group down the road. It does mean that we need to take a closer look at ourselves, what we believe, and why. Children are not born hating one another, hating someone different from them. Children have to be taught to hate.

Let me give you a little background on my family. Here is a picture of myself.....

## *Symphonies*

I am white. I was adopted by an all-white family. My parents had three children; a few years later my parents adopted a boy who is biracial. Then another few years later I was born, and my parents adopted me.

Growing up, our family lived on the east side of our street. Across the street from us, on the west side of the street, lived a black family who had adopted a white child. With this upbringing, I think I have a different view on race.

I do not concentrate on the color or ethnicity or race of a person-I concentrate on the person.

I have heard insensitive jokes in the past, and blatant racially insensitive comments.

I find it is best to take myself out of the situation when that happens.

I will not tolerate such comments from anyone.

Racism, colorism, and biases are found the world over.

For us to really be in a "post-racist" society, we need to be able to be comfortable enough to admit our biases and beliefs and talk about these things with one another, across racial backgrounds, across misconceptions.

We are more alike than we are different.

# Lonely Fedora                  August 27, 2013

Lonely fedora, on the side of the road.

How did you get there? Why are you on the side of the road?

Did someone lose you? Did you blow away in a breeze?

Does your owner know you are lost?

I remember seeing you in classic Hollywood.

You have appeared in many classic movies.

I remember seeing you on Humphrey Bogart in "Casablanca", Gene Kelly in "Singing in the Rain", on Judy Garland in "Summer Stock." Iconic images in cinema.

The fedora hat. The epitome of class and style.

I have had many hats in my time. (I look very good in hats.)

I have always wanted a fedora. But I have never owned one.

It feels so wrong, to see you discarded, in a heap, on the side of the road.

If I were your owner, you would be the cherished piece in my hat collection.

I hope your owner comes back for you....
      ......lonely fedora.......

            ..................on the side of the road.

*Symphonies*

## The Birth of a Book     September 4, 2013

Time is going by so fast. This year, in particular, has gone by in a blur. I cannot believe that it is already September.

In thinking about my business, I have come a long way.
I began the year with the goal of founding my own publishing company, to publish my writings. It was a dream that I did not know if I could achieve. In April of this year I achieved that goal. My publishing company, La Luna Press is up and running.

After the establishment of the business, I then set my sights on all of the proper things one has to do when starting a business. Paperwork has to be filed for tax purposes, a bank account must be established for the business, etc. Once those things were done, I then set my sights on publishing.

I have poetry on two blogs, this one as well as my first blog, Words of Hope. In one sense, the hard part is over; I have already written the poetry to go in the books. In another sense, the hard part had just begun.

I went back to my very first writings, put them in chronological order, and created a collection of poetry. Since I have written so much poetry in the last two years, I decided to create two collections of poetry. (With my writings this year, I could have a third!) On my first blog, I wrote poetry in English and Spanish. Therefore, my first books will be my poetry, in two collections, in both Spanish and English. I will have them available in an electronic book version as well. (That makes eight books!)

The next step in the process is editing the books. It is truly an art, to get the right view of the page. The typeset, the spacing, all make a huge difference to the final product. There are many individuals and companies who work as editors, which charge for their services. I am fortunate in that I have one of my sisters helping me edit the books. We are working on book one. It is about 90% done.

While she worked on editing the first book, I then began to design a website for my company. The site is live now; you can find it here: www.lalunapress.com

In addition to building the website, I designed the covers for the books. I know how to create calendars, flyers, greeting cards on a computer. I was confident in my skills and knew it would be easy for me to create a book cover. Or so I thought. It took much trial and error, research, consulting with relatives, friends, photographers, magicians. After many months, I finally have the covers of the books completed, and in the correct format.

You might be reading this and asking yourself, "What's next?" The next step is to finalize the editing of book one, and use that as a model for the other three. After that, well…There are about 1,000 steps to publishing a book, and I am learning as I go. I am not only launching one book, I'm launching eight. It is a daunting task, to say the least. However, I am up to the challenge. I feel I am at the halfway point in this endeavor. I am anxious to reach my destination. That being said, I am enjoying the journey.

They say that seeing a creative project come to fruition is the equivalent of giving birth. When I began this process, I never knew what went in to the birth of a book.

*Symphonies*

## The Heart                September 12, 2013

I saw a heart the other day. It was just sitting in the road.

I do not know how I noticed it. I suppose I was in the right place at the right time. There it was-a small brown leaf, in the shape of a heart. Lying on the pavement. I do not know what it was doing there, lying in the road. I do not know how it got there. I do not know whose heart it was.

I thought to myself, why would a heart be in the middle of the road? Why did I see it? Was I meant to see this heart? Was it there for anyone to see? What is its significance? Had someone lost it? Was it waiting to be found? Did I find the heart? Or, did it find me? In thinking about the significance of the heart, the answer is simple-love. Love, like air, is all around us. Love is like energy; it is an ever flowing current of power that has no limits or boundaries. Love cannot be destroyed. Love envelops us into itself.

We do not have to find love. We are a part of love. As often happens, we do not have to look for love. Love finds us.
We are found when we least expect it.

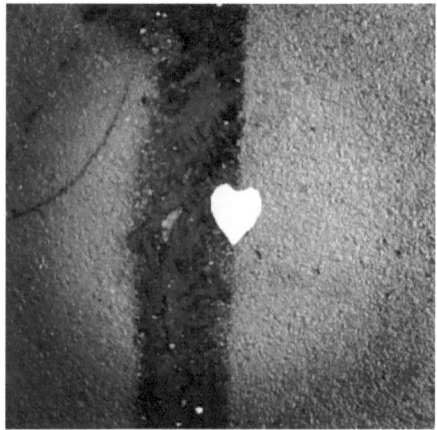

*"The Heart" by Esperanza Habla*

## Scars and Storms       September 20, 2013

About six weeks ago, my kittens broke a small glass tray. I gathered all of the glass I could, and then I used my vacuum cleaner to pick up the smaller shards of glass. A few weeks later, I was sitting on the floor, addressing an envelope. I got up from the floor, and put in a movie I wanted to watch. I then noticed a strange sensation; I looked down to find that I was bleeding profusely from my right leg.

My leg had made contact with an errant shard of glass, still buried in the carpet, from when the kittens had broken the small glass tray. As a result, I was left with a three inch gash below my right knee. The cut was jagged and quite deep. I washed the wound with soap and water. I covered the wound in ointment, gauze and surgical tape. Three weeks later, the wound has healed. A scar has formed.

I awoke last night to the sound of booming thunder, followed seconds later by blinding lightening. The thunder frightened me; it was terribly loud and seemed to shake the whole house. I then heard the meow of one of the kittens. She was on the ledge above my bed, absolutely terrified.

I called out to her; she meowed again. I could tell that she was scared. She needed reassurance, to know that everything would be alright. I called her name, she meowed back. I reached up and began to pet her. She began to purr. I assured her that she would be fine. We would all be fine. Morning came, the storm passed. All was right with the world.

It is an interesting evolution, the process of healing. If we know the storm is coming, we make preparations for it. However, many times we have no warning. Accidents happen. People get hurt. The storm takes us by surprise. We have no time to prepare. We are left searching for answers, devastated by what has happened.

I have a few friends that are mending their own wounds, emotional scars, straining to recover from the of the devastating events in their lives, to pick up the pieces from their storms. To those friends:


The storm you are currently experiencing will pass.

You are already working in the process of healing.

You must help yourself.

Your survival is up to you.

You survived the injury.

You survived the storm.

You are here.

You survived.

Wear your scars proudly.

Tell your tale of survival.

When you see another who is going through a storm, has suffered a terrible hurt, throw them a life preserver.

Be there for others as they were there for you.

# Tolerance                    September 26, 2013

Today marks the One Hundred Thousand Poets for Change. This is a global event, which also includes musicians, performance artists, mimes, poets, and artists of every description. Over 100 countries are participating, through poetry readings, demonstrations, festivals, and countless other celebrations. The goal of this event is to bring about tangible, positive change, to benefit our communities and our world.

In thinking about this event, I have been thinking about the issues I am passionate about. To be completely honest, I have given this event much thought. There are not many topics that I am passionate about that I have not already written about. I have finally decided on a topic, one that is similar to other poems I have written, that of tolerance.

Tolerance is defined as:
> **"a fair, objective...attitude toward those whose opinions, practices, race, religion, nationality, etc., differ from one's own; freedom from bigotry."**
> (Wikipedia definition)

Tolerance is a much needed attribute in this world. We must have it in this world, both within ourselves and within our relationships with others.

I find that I cannot talk about tolerance without talking about its opposite, intolerance. Let me give you an example...

A few months ago, I had a discussion with a co-worker about marriage equality. My position is that I am in favor or equal rights for all, regardless of age or gender, regardless of religious beliefs or lack thereof, regardless of color or sexual orientation. The statements my co-worker made let me know that he definitely felt the opposite. I expressed my opinion, he expressed his. When he was done talking, I said to him:

> **"I can tell you are passionate about this issue.**
> **I do not agree with anything you just said.**
> **But I thank you for sharing your views with me."**

He then continued to talk to me, to try to convince me that I was wrong and that he was right. I again told him I disagreed, and again thanked him for telling me how he felt. I did not agree with my co-worker's views, but I did not try to change them; I was tolerant of his views and opinions and beliefs. He however was intolerant of my views and opinions and beliefs, and tried to change my stance on the issue to match his.

Another example: I have been learning the Spanish language for three years now. To look at me, you would not think I know a word of Spanish. But I am learning Spanish, and use it every day to speak with clients in my library. It makes me proud that I can help bridge the language gap in service, both in advertisements for library programming, and in communicating one on one with a client. I find that people are surprised to learn that I know Spanish; the clients who I have helped in Spanish are always very appreciative for the help, and for the service. I have had non-Spanish speaking clients in my library notice my helping other clients in Spanish. I had one person tell me:

> **"That's wonderful that you can speak Spanish**
> **and help them in their language."**

Another person told me,

> **"They are in our country now;**
> **they need to speak our language."**

That statement makes me cringe every time I hear it (or when I hear any other statement like it.) To be clear, The United States does not have an official language.

My country was originally founded by English citizens fleeing from religious persecution. With the exception of the native tribes that inhabited this land, all of us came to the United States from somewhere. We are a nation of immigrants. Some came here by choice, some came here through enslavement. We all came to this land from somewhere. Today, I find that many Americans are intolerant towards people emigrating here from other nations, speaking different languages, practicing different religions and cultures.

There is one form of intolerance that seems to be global…differences. It appears that we, as a human race, are addicted to differences. We seem to be stuck on labels:

    **"Liberal" "Conservative" "Christian" "Jewish"**
    **"Muslim" "Buddhist" "Republican" "Democrat"**
    **"Gay" "Straight" "Transgender" "Bi-sexual"**
    **"American" "Arab" "Serbian" "Croatian"**
    **"White" "Black" "Latino" "Asian"**
    **"Fat" "Thin" "Beautiful" "Ugly"**

These labels do not define human beings-they divide us. We make these labels to set us apart from others. We use words like "us" and "them" and "they", when in reality we are "us."

Tolerance is a concept that must be practiced globally. However, we cannot change the world without first changing ourselves. Tolerance must begin with each one of us, as individuals. In thinking about myself, I find that I am a very tolerant person. There are many things I tolerate. However, there are many things I cannot-and will

not tolerate. I cannot tolerate unkindness. I will not tolerate disrespect. I cannot tolerate racism. I will not tolerate bigotry. I cannot tolerate xenophobia. I will not tolerate cruelty to animals. I cannot tolerate homophobia.
I will not tolerate hate.

When tolerance is practiced within ourselves, we must then apply it in our relationships with others. The end result, the impact of such a practice, will be global. But it can only start, and it must start, with each one of us.

> *"We need to promote greater tolerance and understanding among the peoples of the world. Nothing can be more dangerous to our efforts to build peace and development than a world divided along religious, ethnic or cultural lines. In each nation, and among all nations, we must work to promote unity based on*
> *our shared humanity."*
> *– Kofi Annan*

> *"In the practice of tolerance,*
> *one's enemy is the best teacher"*
> *-the Dalai Lama*

> *"Human diversity makes tolerance more than a virtue; it makes it a requirement for survival."*
> *- René Dubos*

> *"The Potter books in general are a prolonged argument for tolerance, a prolonged plea for an end to bigotry."*
> *-J.K. Rowling*

*"Tolerance, a term which we sometimes use in place of the words respect, mercy, generosity, or forbearance, is the most essential element of moral systems; it is a very important source of spiritual discipline and a celestial virtue of perfected people."*
*- M. Fethullah Gülen*

*"...if we are open and we prepare for promoting dialogue and love, and a better understanding of each other, and tolerance and so forth, that's what the world will become, a more tolerant, loving place."*
*- Russell Simmons*

*"Through the centuries, the history of peoples is but a lesson in mutual tolerance."*
*-Emil Zola*

*"Nuremberg taught me that creating a world of tolerance and compassion would be a long and arduous task. And I also learned that if we did not devote ourselves to developing effective world law, the same cruel mentality that made the Holocaust possible might one day destroy the entire human race."*
*-Benjamin Ferencz, Nuremberg prosecutor.*

# About the Author

Esperanza Habla is the pen name of the Indigo Poet of the Moon. She began her writing career in 2010. Her blog, "Letters to the Moon", has garnered a readership of more than eighty-five countries worldwide.

In 2013 Esperanza founded her own publishing company, La Luna Press, L.L.C. Her first book of poetry, "I am Hope", was published in April of 2015.

Esperanza holds a degree in Music History and Literature from Marian University. She has been featured in the Poetry Daily and has received a nomination for the Indiana Authors Award in 2015 and 2016.

This is her third book of poetry published in English.

www.lalunapress.com
www.esperanzahabla.com

# Other publications from La Luna Press:

## www.lalunapress.com

www.ingramcontent.com/pod-product-compliance
Lightning Source LLC
Chambersburg PA
CBHW041403090426
42743CB00006B/139